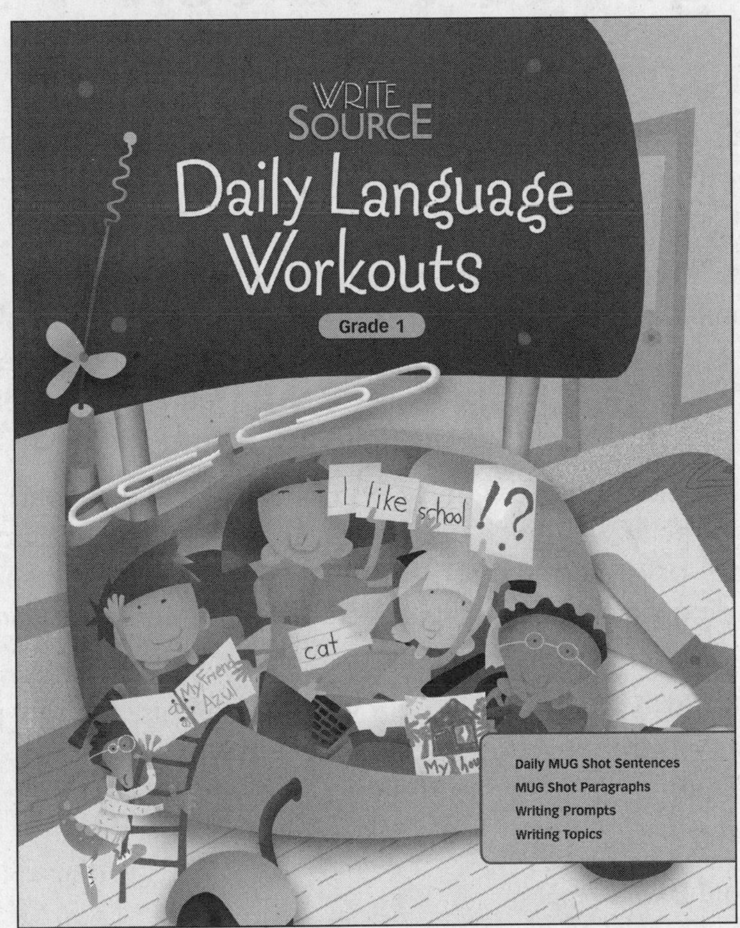

Daily language and writing practice for

Grade 1

WRITE SOURCE®

GREAT SOURCE EDUCATION GROUP
a Houghton Mifflin Company
Wilmington, Massachusetts
www.greatsource.com

A Few Words About *Daily Language Workouts 1*

Before you begin . . .

The activities in this book are intended to be used for group instruction on a daily basis. They will help your students develop basic writing and language skills. You'll find three types of exercises on the following pages:

MUG Shot Sentences There are 180 sentences highlighting **m**echanics, **u**sage, and/or **g**rammar (MUG), one for each day of the school year. The first 4 weeks call for interactive, teacher-directed writing. For the next 23 weeks, focused sentences usually concentrate on one skill per week. For the final 9 weeks, sentences present a mixed review, and students are asked to correct several types of errors in each sentence.

MUG Shot Paragraphs There are 18 weekly paragraphs for the second semester. The first 9 correspond directly with each week's MUG Shot sentences, focusing on the same mechanics, usage, or grammar error. The final 9 paragraphs present a mixed review of the proofreading and editing skills covered during the corresponding weeks of sentences.

Daily Writing Practice This section begins with writing prompts, thought-provoking topics and graphics designed to inspire expository, narrative, descriptive, persuasive, and creative writing. Next, a discussion of daily journal writing introduces the lists of intriguing writing topics.

Authors: Pat Sebranek and Dave Kemper

Printed in the United States of America

International Standard Book Number: 978-0-669-53794-9

7 8 9 10 -POO- 10 09

Contents

Editing and Proofreading Marks

These symbols may be used to correct MUG Shot sentences and paragraphs.

Add a letter.	∧	two trees (s inserted with ∧)
Add a word or words.	∧	take them home (them inserted with ∧)
Add a comma.	∧ with ,	Troy, Michigan
Add a period.	⊙	Mrs⊙
Add a question mark.	∧ with ?	How about you?
Add an exclamation point.	∧ with !	That's amazing!
Capitalize a letter.	≡	iowa (≡ under i)
Add an apostrophe.	∨ with '	Bill's coat

MUG Shot Sentences

The MUG Shot sentences are designed to be used on a daily basis as a quick and efficient way to introduce or review mechanics, usage, and grammar. Each sentence can be presented on a chalkboard, and then corrected and discussed in 3 to 5 minutes.

MUG Shot Sentence Organizer

Name: ______________________ Date: ____________

Corrected Sentence:

Corrected Sentence:

Corrected Sentence:

Corrected Sentence:

Corrected Sentence:

Implementation and Evaluation

The first 4 weeks of MUG Shot sentences are simple interactive writing exercises. The next 23 weeks are focused sentences covering one proofreading skill per week. The remaining 9 weeks of MUG Shot sentences provide mixed reviews of a selection of proofreading skills in each sentence.

Implementation

Write the MUG Shot sentence on the board. Read it aloud to be sure students understand it. Then you or a student should write the correction on the board as a volunteer provides it. If you wish, have students write the corrected form on their paper, in their notebooks, or on copies of page 2, "MUG Shot Sentence Organizer," provided for them. You may choose instead to write the sentence on the board at the beginning of the class period, allowing time for students to read the sentence silently. Read the sentence aloud before actual work begins. As a class, discuss the reasons for each correction. Each Friday, review the week's MUG Shots. During the second semester, consider assigning the corresponding MUG Shot paragraph. (See page 81.)

Evaluation

The best evaluation takes place in the context of your students' daily writing. Use observation and short conferences to do your evaluations.

Week 1: Interactive Sentences (Names)

- **Writing Sentences**

My name is ______________________________.

- **Writing Sentences**

It is nice to meet you, ____________________.

- **Writing Sentences**

I see ______________________________.

- **Writing Sentences**

Where is ______________________________?

- **Writing Sentences**

______________________________ is my friend.

Week 1: Completed Sentences (sample answers)

- **Writing Sentences**

My name is Jenny.

- **Writing Sentences**

It is nice to meet you, Maggie.

- **Writing Sentences**

I see Sloan.

- **Writing Sentences**

Where is Lionel?

- **Writing Sentences**

Aubrey is my friend.

Week 2: Interactive Sentences (Names)

- **Writing Sentences**

_______________ is my name.

- **Writing Sentences**

I play with _______________ .

- **Writing Sentences**

_______________ helps me.

- **Writing Sentences**

When is _______________ coming?

- **Writing Sentences**

Here comes _______________ .

Week 2: Completed Sentences (sample answers)

- **Writing Sentences**

Derek is my name.

- **Writing Sentences**

I play with Bryant.

- **Writing Sentences**

Terron helps me.

- **Writing Sentences**

When is Julia coming?

- **Writing Sentences**

Here comes Kelsey.

Week 3: Interactive Sentences (Colors)

- **Writing Sentences**

I like the color ______________________.

- **Writing Sentences**

______________________ is a bright color.

- **Writing Sentences**

______________________ is a pretty color.

- **Writing Sentences**

Some birds are ______________________.

- **Writing Sentences**

Leaves can be ______________________

or ______________________.

Week 3: Completed Sentences (sample answers)

Writing Sentences

I like the color blue.

Writing Sentences

Yellow is a bright color.

Writing Sentences

Pink is a pretty color.

Writing Sentences

Some birds are red.

Writing Sentences

Leaves can be green

or gold.

Week 4: Interactive Sentences (Colors)

- **Writing Sentences**

I have ______________________________ eyes.

- **Writing Sentences**

Grass is ______________________________ .

- **Writing Sentences**

The sky is ______________________________ .

- **Writing Sentences**

Some flowers are ______________________________ .

- **Writing Sentences**

I like ______________________________ and

______________________________ !

Week 4: Completed Sentences (sample answers)

- **Writing Sentences**

I have brown eyes.

- **Writing Sentences**

Grass is green.

- **Writing Sentences**

The sky is blue.

- **Writing Sentences**

Some flowers are purple.

- **Writing Sentences**

I like red and yellow!

Week 5: Focused Sentences

- **Period at the End of a Telling Sentence**

  My classroom has tables and desks

- **Period at the End of a Telling Sentence**

  I see many students

- **Period at the End of a Telling Sentence**

  Here is my desk

- **Period at the End of a Telling Sentence**

  I see a flag

- **Period at the End of a Telling Sentence**

  My class has a goldfish

Week 5: Corrected Sentences

- **Period at the End of a Telling Sentence**

  My classroom has tables and desks⊙

- **Period at the End of a Telling Sentence**

  I see many students⊙

- **Period at the End of a Telling Sentence**

  Here is my desk⊙

- **Period at the End of a Telling Sentence**

  I see a flag⊙

- **Period at the End of a Telling Sentence**

  My class has a goldfish⊙

Week 6: Focused Sentences

- **Question Mark at the End of an Asking Sentence**

  May we go to the library

- **Question Mark at the End of an Asking Sentence**

  What will we read

- **Question Mark at the End of an Asking Sentence**

  Have we read this story

- **Question Mark at the End of an Asking Sentence**

  Is it about a dog

- **Question Mark at the End of an Asking Sentence**

  Will I like the story

Week 6: Corrected Sentences

- **Question Mark at the End of an Asking Sentence**

May we go to the library?

- **Question Mark at the End of an Asking Sentence**

What will we read?

- **Question Mark at the End of an Asking Sentence**

Have we read this story?

- **Question Mark at the End of an Asking Sentence**

Is it about a dog?

- **Question Mark at the End of an Asking Sentence**

Will I like the story?

Week 7: Focused Sentences

- **Exclamation Point at the End of an Exciting Sentence**

  The school picnic is finally here

- **Exclamation Point at the End of an Exciting Sentence**

  Here comes the bus

- **Exclamation Point at the End of an Exciting Sentence**

  One, two, three, everybody climb aboard

- **Exclamation Point at the End of an Exciting Sentence**

  This is a great day for races and games

- **Exclamation Point at the End of an Exciting Sentence**

  Get ready, get set, go

Week 7: Corrected Sentences

- **Exclamation Point at the End of an Exciting Sentence**

  The school picnic is finally here!

- **Exclamation Point at the End of an Exciting Sentence**

  Here comes the bus!

- **Exclamation Point at the End of an Exciting Sentence**

  One, two, three, everybody climb aboard!

- **Exclamation Point at the End of an Exciting Sentence**

  This is a great day for races and games!

- **Exclamation Point at the End of an Exciting Sentence**

  Get ready, get set, go!

Week 8: Focused Sentences

- **Capital Letter for the First Word in a Sentence**

  after school, I play soccer.

- **Capital Letter for the First Word in a Sentence**

  boys and girls play on the team.

- **Capital Letter for the First Word in a Sentence**

  my dad is the coach.

- **Capital Letter for the First Word in a Sentence**

  he knows the soccer rules.

- **Capital Letter for the First Word in a Sentence**

  it is fun to run and play.

Week 8: Corrected Sentences

- **Capital Letter for the First Word in a Sentence**

A
after school, I play soccer.

- **Capital Letter for the First Word in a Sentence**

B
boys and girls play on the team.

- **Capital Letter for the First Word in a Sentence**

M
my dad is the coach.

- **Capital Letter for the First Word in a Sentence**

H
he knows the soccer rules.

- **Capital Letter for the First Word in a Sentence**

I
it is fun to run and play.

Week 9: Focused Sentences

- **Capital Letters for Special Names**

  We went to a museum in oklahoma.

- **Capital Letters for Special Names**

  In one room, keesha heard music.

- **Capital Letters for Special Names**

  At noon, willie tried new foods.

- **Capital Letters for Special Names**

  Then sandra touched a snake's skin!

- **Capital Letters for Special Names**

  Later, paul looked at a big dinosaur tooth.

Week 9: Corrected Sentences

- **Capital Letters for Special Names**

  We went to a museum in oklahoma. (O)

- **Capital Letters for Special Names**

  In one room, keesha heard music. (K)

- **Capital Letters for Special Names**

  At noon, willie tried new foods. (W)

- **Capital Letters for Special Names**

  Then sandra touched a snake's skin! (S)

- **Capital Letters for Special Names**

  Later, paul looked at a big dinosaur tooth. (P)

Week 10: Focused Sentences

- **Capital Letter for the Word *I***

i am going to school!

- **Capital Letter for the Word *I***

Do i need anything?

- **Capital Letter for the Word *I***

Yes, i need a backpack.

- **Capital Letter for the Word *I***

Today i am going to a museum.

- **Capital Letter for the Word *I***

You and i will see many things.

Week 10: Corrected Sentences

- **Capital Letter for the Word *I***

I
i am going to school!

- **Capital Letter for the Word *I***

I
Do i need anything?

- **Capital Letter for the Word *I***

I
Yes, i need a backpack.

- **Capital Letter for the Word *I***

I
Today i am going to a museum.

- **Capital Letter for the Word *I***

I
You and i will see many things.

Week 11: Capitalization Review Sentences

- **Capital Letters for First Words, Special Names, and the Word *I***

This is my cousin john.

- **Capital Letters for First Words, Special Names, and the Word *I***

He lives in texas.

- **Capital Letters for First Words, Special Names, and the Word *I***

once, I went to visit him.

- **Capital Letters for First Words, Special Names, and the Word *I***

We saw the Gulf of mexico.

- **Capital Letters for First Words, Special Names, and the Word *I***

John and i jumped in the waves.

Week 11: Corrected Sentences

- **Capital Letters for First Words, Special Names, and the Word *I***

This is my cousin john. (J)

- **Capital Letters for First Words, Special Names, and the Word *I***

He lives in texas. (T)

- **Capital Letters for First Words, Special Names, and the Word *I***

once, I went to visit him. (O)

- **Capital Letters for First Words, Special Names, and the Word *I***

We saw the Gulf of mexico. (M)

- **Capital Letters for First Words, Special Names, and the Word *I***

John and i jumped in the waves. (I)

Week 12: Focused Sentences

- **Plurals That Add -*s***

  We are studying mammal.

- **Plurals That Add -*s***

  Mother feed their babies milk.

- **Plurals That Add -*s***

  Baby bears are called cub.

- **Plurals That Add -*s***

  Baby goats are called kid.

- **Plurals That Add -*s***

  Horses have foal.

Week 12: Corrected Sentences

- **Plurals That Add -*s***

  We are studying mammal^s.

- **Plurals That Add -*s***

  Mother^s feed their babies milk.

- **Plurals That Add -*s***

  Baby bears are called cub^s.

- **Plurals That Add -*s***

  Baby goats are called kid^s.

- **Plurals That Add -*s***

  Horses have foal^s.

Week 13: Focused Sentences

- **Period at the End of a Telling Sentence**

  We go to town

- **Period at the End of a Telling Sentence**

  We stop at a store

- **Period at the End of a Telling Sentence**

  It is a grocery store

- **Period at the End of a Telling Sentence**

  We get milk and bread

- **Period at the End of a Telling Sentence**

  We also get some carrot sticks

Week 13: Corrected Sentences

- **Period at the End of a Telling Sentence**

  We go to town.

- **Period at the End of a Telling Sentence**

  We stop at a store.

- **Period at the End of a Telling Sentence**

  It is a grocery store.

- **Period at the End of a Telling Sentence**

  We get milk and bread.

- **Period at the End of a Telling Sentence**

  We also get some carrot sticks.

Week 14: Focused Sentences

- **Period After an Abbreviation**

  Ms Brown likes being our principal.

- **Period After an Abbreviation**

  Ms Chang works in the school office.

- **Period After an Abbreviation**

  Mr Diaz is our librarian.

- **Period After an Abbreviation**

  Our head cook is Mrs Green.

- **Period After an Abbreviation**

  Mr Jones cleans our school.

Week 14: Corrected Sentences

- **Period After an Abbreviation**

Ms⨀Brown likes being our principal.

- **Period After an Abbreviation**

Ms⨀Chang works in the school office.

- **Period After an Abbreviation**

Mr⨀Diaz is our librarian.

- **Period After an Abbreviation**

Our head cook is Mrs⨀Green.

- **Period After an Abbreviation**

Mr⨀Jones cleans our school.

Week 15: Focused Sentences

- **Question Mark at the End of an Asking Sentence**

  Do you see the elephants

- **Question Mark at the End of an Asking Sentence**

  Why are the clowns running

- **Question Mark at the End of an Asking Sentence**

  Are the clowns getting wet

- **Question Mark at the End of an Asking Sentence**

  Is it starting to rain

- **Question Mark at the End of an Asking Sentence**

  Are the elephants spraying water

Week 15: Corrected Sentences

- **Question Mark at the End of an Asking Sentence**

Do you see the elephants?

- **Question Mark at the End of an Asking Sentence**

Why are the clowns running?

- **Question Mark at the End of an Asking Sentence**

Are the clowns getting wet?

- **Question Mark at the End of an Asking Sentence**

Is it starting to rain?

- **Question Mark at the End of an Asking Sentence**

Are the elephants spraying water?

Week 16: Focused Sentences

- **Exclamation Point at the End of an Exciting Sentence**

  Somebody help me

- **Exclamation Point at the End of an Exciting Sentence**

  My backpack is lost

- **Exclamation Point at the End of an Exciting Sentence**

  I don't want to be late

- **Exclamation Point at the End of an Exciting Sentence**

  Help, Dad

- **Exclamation Point at the End of an Exciting Sentence**

  You're my hero

Week 16: Corrected Sentences

- **Exclamation Point at the End of an Exciting Sentence**

  Somebody help me!

- **Exclamation Point at the End of an Exciting Sentence**

  My backpack is lost!

- **Exclamation Point at the End of an Exciting Sentence**

  I don't want to be late!

- **Exclamation Point at the End of an Exciting Sentence**

  Help, Dad!

- **Exclamation Point at the End of an Exciting Sentence**

  You're my hero!

Week 17: Punctuation Review Sentences

- **Period, Question Mark, Exclamation Point at the End of a Sentence**

  Did you see the fish jump

- **Period, Question Mark, Exclamation Point at the End of a Sentence**

  It made a big splash

- **Period, Question Mark, Exclamation Point at the End of a Sentence**

  I think it was a sunfish

- **Period, Question Mark, Exclamation Point at the End of a Sentence**

  Look what I caught

- **Period, Question Mark, Exclamation Point at the End of a Sentence**

  Do you want to go fishing

Week 17: Corrected Sentences

- **Period, Question Mark, Exclamation Point at the End of a Sentence**

Did you see the fish jump?

- **Period, Question Mark, Exclamation Point at the End of a Sentence**

It made a big splash!

- **Period, Question Mark, Exclamation Point at the End of a Sentence**

I think it was a sunfish.

- **Period, Question Mark, Exclamation Point at the End of a Sentence**

Look what I caught!

- **Period, Question Mark, Exclamation Point at the End of a Sentence**

Do you want to go fishing?

Week 18: Focused Sentences

- **Comma After the Greeting and the Closing in a Letter**

Dear Bernie

I saw your new bike. It is cool! Did you get a new helmet, too?

Your friend

Sean

- **Comma After the Greeting and the Closing in a Letter**

Dear Uncle Chang

I went to the beach. I collected pretty shells. Will you visit us soon? Please write back.

Your niece

Lin

- **Comma After the Greeting and the Closing in a Letter**

Dear Grandpa

Thanks for taking me fishing. Let's go again!

Love

Stuart

Week 18 (continued)

- **Comma After the Greeting and the Closing in a Letter**

Dear Grammie

Hi! Do you know what happened today? I got a prize at school. I got a new book. It is about a boy and his horse.

Love

Manny

- **Comma After the Greeting and the Closing in a Letter**

Dear Mom

I'm having fun at Uncle Steve's house. We had a picnic today. We went swimming at the pool.

Love

Marty

Week 18: Corrected Sentences

- **Comma After the Greeting and the Closing in a Letter**

Dear Bernie,

I saw your new bike. It is cool! Did you get a new helmet, too?

Your friend,
Sean

- **Comma After the Greeting and the Closing in a Letter**

Dear Uncle Chang,

I went to the beach. I collected pretty shells. Will you visit us soon? Please write back.

Your niece,
Lin

- **Comma After the Greeting and the Closing in a Letter**

Dear Grandpa,

Thanks for taking me fishing. Let's go again!

Love,
Stuart

Week 18: Corrected Sentences (continued)

- **Comma After the Greeting and the Closing in a Letter**

Dear Grammie‸,

Hi! Do you know what happened today? I got a prize at school. I got a new book. It is about a boy and his horse.

Love‸,
Manny

- **Comma After the Greeting and the Closing in a Letter**

Dear Mom‸,

I'm having fun at Uncle Steve's house. We had a picnic today. We went swimming at the pool.

Love‸,
Marty

Week 19: Focused Sentences

- **Comma Between the Day and the Year**

  We moved to our new house on January 2 2004.

- **Comma Between the Day and the Year**

  Our puppy was born on February 13 2006.

- **Comma Between the Day and the Year**

  We went to the ocean on March 22 2005.

- **Comma Between the Day and the Year**

  Sara was six years old on April 16 2006.

- **Comma Between the Day and the Year**

  My dad was born on May 6 1974.

Week 19: Corrected Sentences

- **Comma Between the Day and the Year**

We moved to our new house on January 2, 2004.

- **Comma Between the Day and the Year**

Our puppy was born on February 13, 2006.

- **Comma Between the Day and the Year**

We went to the ocean on March 22, 2005.

- **Comma Between the Day and the Year**

Sara was six years old on April 16, 2006.

- **Comma Between the Day and the Year**

My dad was born on May 6, 1974.

Week 20: Focused Sentences

- **Comma Between Words in a Series**

  I like to run jump and climb during recess.

- **Comma Between Words in a Series**

  Sometimes I paint draw or color.

- **Comma Between Words in a Series**

  I use crayons scissors and glue in art class.

- **Comma Between Words in a Series**

  I like waffles fruit and milk for breakfast.

- **Comma Between Words in a Series**

  Grandma Grandpa and Uncle Chas visited us.

Week 20: Corrected Sentences

- **Comma Between Words in a Series**

I like to run, jump, and climb during recess.

- **Comma Between Words in a Series**

Sometimes I paint, draw, or color.

- **Comma Between Words in a Series**

I use crayons, scissors, and glue in art class.

- **Comma Between Words in a Series**

I like waffles, fruit, and milk for breakfast.

- **Comma Between Words in a Series**

Grandma, Grandpa, and Uncle Chas visited us.

Week 21: Focused Sentences

- **Apostrophe to Make a Contraction**

  Im sure I saw a deer.

- **Apostrophe to Make a Contraction**

  Look, its moving!

- **Apostrophe to Make a Contraction**

  The deer didnt see me.

- **Apostrophe to Make a Contraction**

  Dont make any sounds.

- **Apostrophe to Make a Contraction**

  Isnt the deer pretty?

Week 21: Corrected Sentences

- **Apostrophe to Make a Contraction**

  I'm sure I saw a deer.

- **Apostrophe to Make a Contraction**

  Look, it's moving!

- **Apostrophe to Make a Contraction**

  The deer didn't see me.

- **Apostrophe to Make a Contraction**

  Don't make any sounds.

- **Apostrophe to Make a Contraction**

  Isn't the deer pretty?

Week 22: Focused Sentences

- **Using the Right Word (to, too, two)**

  Can you go ________________ a movie with me?

- **Using the Right Word (to, too, two)**

  It is about ________________ tigers.

- **Using the Right Word (buy, by)**

  Mom will ________________ the tickets.

- **Using the Right Word (buy, by)**

  The theater is ________________ my house.

- **Using the Right Word (to, too, two)**

  Ask your brother to come, ________________ .

Week 22: Corrected Sentences

- **Using the Right Word (to, too, two)**

Can you go ___to___ a movie with me?

- **Using the Right Word (to, too, two)**

It is about ___two___ tigers.

- **Using the Right Word (buy, by)**

Mom will ___buy___ the tickets.

- **Using the Right Word (buy, by)**

The theater is ___by___ my house.

- **Using the Right Word (to, too, two)**

Ask your brother to come, ___too___ .

Week 23: Focused Sentences

- **Using the Right Word (dear, deer)**

My grandma took me to a ________________ park.

- **Using the Right Word (road, rode)**

We ________________ in the car for a long time.

- **Using the Right Word (dear, deer)**

Then we fed the ________________ .

- **Using the Right Word (road, rode)**

The ________________ was bumpy.

- **Using the Right Word (dear, deer)**

I wrote a note to thank my ________________ grandma.

Week 23: Corrected Sentences

- **Using the Right Word (dear, deer)**

My grandma took me to a ___deer___ park.

- **Using the Right Word (road, rode)**

We ___rode___ in the car for a long time.

- **Using the Right Word (dear, deer)**

Then we fed the ___deer___ .

- **Using the Right Word (road, rode)**

The ___road___ was bumpy.

- **Using the Right Word (dear, deer)**

I wrote a note to thank my ___dear___ grandma.

Week 24: Focused Sentences

- **Using the Right Word (blew, blue)**

The summer sky was the color ________________ .

- **Using the Right Word (for, four)**

I looked ________________ grasshoppers.

- **Using the Right Word (blew, blue)**

The wind ________________ the grass.

- **Using the Right Word (for, four)**

I saw ________________ bees on one flower.

- **Using the Right Word (for, four)**

I pulled weeds ________________ my mom.

Week 24: Corrected Sentences

- **Using the Right Word (blew, blue)**

The summer sky was the color blue.

- **Using the Right Word (for, four)**

I looked for grasshoppers.

- **Using the Right Word (blew, blue)**

The wind blew the grass.

- **Using the Right Word (for, four)**

I saw four bees on one flower.

- **Using the Right Word (for, four)**

I pulled weeds for my mom.

Week 25: Focused Sentences

- **Using the Right Word (red, read)**

I ________________ a book about fire trucks.

- **Using the Right Word (red, read)**

Some fire trucks are ________________ .

- **Using the Right Word (know, no)**

Did you ________________ that?

- **Using the Right Word (Know, No)**

My friend said, "________________."

- **Using the Right Word (red, read)**

I like the shiny ________________ fire trucks.

Week 25: Corrected Sentences

- **Using the Right Word (red, read)**

I ___read___ a book about fire trucks.

- **Using the Right Word (red, read)**

Some fire trucks are ___red___.

- **Using the Right Word (know, no)**

Did you ___know___ that?

- **Using the Right Word (Know, No)**

My friend said, "___No___."

- **Using the Right Word (red, read)**

I like the shiny ___red___ fire trucks.

Week 26: Focused Sentences

- **Using the Right Word (Hear, Here)**

  ____________ comes a parade!

- **Using the Right Word (hear, here)**

  Do you ____________ the band?

- **Using the Right Word (ate, eight)**

  There are ____________ drums.

- **Using the Right Word (hear, here)**

  Look, ____________ come dancers.

- **Using the Right Word (ate, eight)**

  We ____________ snacks after the parade.

Week 26: Corrected Sentences

- **Using the Right Word (Hear, Here)**

Here comes a parade!

- **Using the Right Word (hear, here)**

Do you hear the band?

- **Using the Right Word (ate, eight)**

There are eight drums.

- **Using the Right Word (hear, here)**

Look, here come dancers.

- **Using the Right Word (ate, eight)**

We ate snacks after the parade.

Week 27: Focused Sentences

- **Using the Right Word (to, two, too)**

I took my dog ________________ the dog show.

- **Using the Right Word (one, won)**

My dog ________________ a prize.

- **Using the Right Word (To, Two, Too)**

________________ judges looked at her.

- **Using the Right Word (One, Won)**

________________ dog barked.

- **Using the Right Word (to, two, too)**

My dog barked, ________________ .

Week 27: Corrected Sentences

- **Using the Right Word (to, two, too)**

I took my dog ___to___ the dog show.

- **Using the Right Word (one, won)**

My dog ___won___ a prize.

- **Using the Right Word (To, Two, Too)**

___Two___ judges looked at her.

- **Using the Right Word (One, Won)**

___One___ dog barked.

- **Using the Right Word (to, two, too)**

My dog barked, ___too___ .

Week 28: Mixed-Review Sentences

- **Capital Letter for the First Word in a Sentence, Using the Right Word**

a squirrel is saving nuts ________________ the winter.
(for, four)

- **Capital Letter for the First Word in a Sentence, Using the Right Word**

the bears ________________ it's time to find a cave.
(know, no)

- **Capital Letter for the First Word in a Sentence, Using the Right Word**

can you ________________ the geese?
(hear, here)

- **Capital Letter for the First Word in a Sentence, Using the Right Word**

turtles get ready for winter, ____________ .
(to, two, too)

- **Capital Letter for the First Word in a Sentence, Using the Right Word**

we watched as ____________ turtles crossed the path.
(for, four)

Week 28: Corrected Sentences

- **Capital Letter for the First Word in a Sentence, Using the Right Word**

A
a squirrel is saving nuts ___for___ the winter.
(for, four)

- **Capital Letter for the First Word in a Sentence, Using the Right Word**

T
the bears ___know___ it's time to find a cave.
(know, no)

- **Capital Letter for the First Word in a Sentence, Using the Right Word**

C
can you ___hear___ the geese?
(hear, here)

- **Capital Letter for the First Word in a Sentence, Using the Right Word**

T
turtles get ready for winter, ___too___ .
(to, two, too)

- **Capital Letter for the First Word in a Sentence, Using the Right Word**

W
we watched as ___four___ turtles crossed the path.
(for, four)

Week 29: Mixed-Review Sentences

- **Period, Question Mark, or Exclamation Point; Capital Letters for Special Names**

  Did you see Greg on monday

- **Period, Question Mark, or Exclamation Point; Capital Letters for Special Names**

  Greg, tim, and I played soccer on Tuesday

- **Period, Question Mark, or Exclamation Point; Capital Letters for Special Names**

  We asked andy to play with us

- **Period, Question Mark, or Exclamation Point; Capital Letters for Special Names**

  Was ray playing with Juan

- **Period, Question Mark, or Exclamation Point; Capital Letters for Special Names**

  Wow, we won our soccer game on thursday

Week 29: Corrected Sentences

- **Period, Question Mark, or Exclamation Point; Capital Letters for Special Names**

  Did you see Greg on monday (M; ?)

- **Period, Question Mark, or Exclamation Point; Capital Letters for Special Names**

  Greg, tim (T), and I played soccer on Tuesday (.)

- **Period, Question Mark, or Exclamation Point; Capital Letters for Special Names**

  We asked andy (A) to play with us (.)

- **Period, Question Mark, or Exclamation Point; Capital Letters for Special Names**

  Was ray (R) playing with Juan (?)

- **Period, Question Mark, or Exclamation Point; Capital Letters for Special Names**

  Wow, we won our soccer game on thursday (T; !)

Week 30: Mixed-Review Sentences

- **Capital Letter for the Word *I*, Question Mark**

  Am i older than you are

- **Capital Letter for the Word *I*, Question Mark**

  May i go to the zoo

- **Capital Letter for the Word *I*, Question Mark**

  Do i have my lunch

- **Capital Letter for the Word *I*, Question Mark**

  Where did i put my shoes

- **Capital Letter for the Word *I*, Question Mark**

  May i play after school

Week 30: Corrected Sentences

- **Capital Letter for the Word *I*, Question Mark**

Am i older than you are (i → I, ?)

- **Capital Letter for the Word *I*, Question Mark**

May i go to the zoo (i → I, ?)

- **Capital Letter for the Word *I*, Question Mark**

Do i have my lunch (i → I, ?)

- **Capital Letter for the Word *I*, Question Mark**

Where did i put my shoes (i → I, ?)

- **Capital Letter for the Word *I*, Question Mark**

May i play after school (i → I, ?)

Week 31: Mixed-Review Sentences

- **Apostrophe to Make a Contraction, Exclamation Point**

  Im going skateboarding today

- **Apostrophe to Make a Contraction, Exclamation Point**

  Its going to be fun

- **Apostrophe to Make a Contraction, Exclamation Point**

  I dont want to stop

- **Apostrophe to Make a Contraction, Exclamation Point**

  Lets go around the block again

- **Apostrophe to Make a Contraction, Exclamation Point**

  I didnt know skateboarding was so much fun

Week 31: Corrected Sentences

- **Apostrophe to Make a Contraction, Exclamation Point**

  I'm going skateboarding today!

- **Apostrophe to Make a Contraction, Exclamation Point**

  It's going to be fun!

- **Apostrophe to Make a Contraction, Exclamation Point**

  I don't want to stop!

- **Apostrophe to Make a Contraction, Exclamation Point**

  Let's go around the block again!

- **Apostrophe to Make a Contraction, Exclamation Point**

  I didn't know skateboarding was so much fun!

Week 32: Mixed-Review Sentences

- **Apostrophe to Make a Contraction, Plurals That Add -*s***

Its time for snack.

- **Apostrophe to Make a Contraction, Plurals That Add -*s***

Im having carrot stick and raisin.

- **Apostrophe to Make a Contraction, Plurals That Add -*s***

Jake didnt bring his grape.

- **Apostrophe to Make a Contraction, Plurals That Add -*s***

Ill share my raisin with him.

- **Apostrophe to Make a Contraction, Plurals That Add -*s***

Tomorrow well all have apple.

Week 32: Corrected Sentences

- **Apostrophe to Make a Contraction, Plurals That Add -*s***

It's time for snacks.

- **Apostrophe to Make a Contraction, Plurals That Add -*s***

I'm having carrot sticks and raisins.

- **Apostrophe to Make a Contraction, Plurals That Add -*s***

Jake didn't bring his grapes.

- **Apostrophe to Make a Contraction, Plurals That Add -*s***

I'll share my raisins with him.

- **Apostrophe to Make a Contraction, Plurals That Add -*s***

Tomorrow we'll all have apples.

Week 33: Mixed-Review Sentences

- **Period After an Abbreviation, Capital Letters for Special Names, Apostrophe to Make a Contraction**

  Mrs deer cried, “Ive lost my fawn!”

- **Period After an Abbreviation, Capital Letters for Special Names, Apostrophe to Make a Contraction**

  “I dont know where she is,” said Mr fox.

- **Period After an Abbreviation, Capital Letters for Special Names, Apostrophe to Make a Contraction**

  Ms bluejay said, “Ill help you look.”

- **Period After an Abbreviation, Capital Letters for Special Names, Apostrophe to Make a Contraction**

  “Isnt that your fawn?” asked Mr mouse.

- **Period After an Abbreviation, Capital Letters for Special Names, Apostrophe to Make a Contraction**

  “I didnt know she was asleep,” said Mrs deer.

Week 33: Corrected Sentences

- **Period After an Abbreviation, Capital Letters for Special Names, Apostrophe to Make a Contraction**

Mrs. Deer cried, "I've lost my fawn!"

- **Period After an Abbreviation, Capital Letters for Special Names, Apostrophe to Make a Contraction**

"I don't know where she is," said Mr. Fox.

- **Period After an Abbreviation, Capital Letters for Special Names, Apostrophe to Make a Contraction**

Ms. Bluejay said, "I'll help you look."

- **Period After an Abbreviation, Capital Letters for Special Names, Apostrophe to Make a Contraction**

"Isn't that your fawn?" asked Mr. Mouse.

- **Period After an Abbreviation, Capital Letters for Special Names, Apostrophe to Make a Contraction**

"I didn't know she was asleep," said Mrs. Deer.

Week 34: Mixed-Review Sentences

- **Using the Right Word, Commas in Letters**

Dear Grandma

My favorite color is ________________ .
(blue, blew)

Love

Maggie

- **Using the Right Word, Commas in Letters**

Dear Maggie

I like your ________________ painting.
(red, read)

Your friend

Henry

- **Using the Right Word, Commas in Letters**

Dear Aunt Jenn

Can you come to my concert at ________________
(ate, eight)
o'clock Friday?

Love

Conall

Week 34 (continued)

- **Using the Right Word, Commas in Letters**

Dear Uncle Mark

Our team ______________ the last game.
(won, one)

Love

Vivian

- **Using the Right Word, Commas in Letters**

Dear Andrew

I ______________ the best book last night.
(red, read)

Your friend

Max

Week 34: Corrected Sentences

- **Using the Right Word, Commas in Letters**

Dear Grandma,

My favorite color is blue.
(blue, blew)

Love,
Maggie

- **Using the Right Word, Commas in Letters**

Dear Maggie,

I like your red painting.
(red, read)

Your friend,
Henry

- **Using the Right Word, Commas in Letters**

Dear Aunt Jenn,

Can you come to my concert at eight o'clock Friday?
(ate, eight)

Love,
Conall

Week 34: Corrected Sentences (continued)

- **Using the Right Word, Commas in Letters**

Dear Uncle Mark,

Our team won the last game.
(won, one)

Love,
Vivian

- **Using the Right Word, Commas in Letters**

Dear Andrew,

I read the best book last night.
(red, read)

Your friend,
Max

Week 35: Mixed-Review Sentences

- **Using the Right Word, Comma Between Words in a Series**

Anna wants a ________________ hat mittens and boots.
(red, read)

- **Using the Right Word, Comma Between Words in a Series**

Will Dad ________________ a bat a glove and a
(buy, by)
catcher's mitt?

- **Using the Right Word, Comma Between Words in a Series**

I want to ________________ monkeys elephants and
(see, sea)
tigers.

- **Using the Right Word, Comma Between Words in a Series**

Miki ________________ an apple a pear and grapes.
(ate, eight)

- **Using the Right Word, Comma Between Words in a Series**

Her ________________ dress had yellow green and
(blue, blew)
orange ribbons.

Week 35: Corrected Sentences

- **Using the Right Word, Comma Between Words in a Series**

Anna wants a red (*red, read*) hat, mittens, and boots.

- **Using the Right Word, Comma Between Words in a Series**

Will Dad buy (*buy, by*) a bat, a glove, and a catcher's mitt?

- **Using the Right Word, Comma Between Words in a Series**

I want to see (*see, sea*) monkeys, elephants, and tigers.

- **Using the Right Word, Comma Between Words in a Series**

Miki ate (*ate, eight*) an apple, a pear, and grapes.

- **Using the Right Word, Comma Between Words in a Series**

Her blue (*blue, blew*) dress had yellow, green, and orange ribbons.

Week 36: Mixed-Review Sentences

- **Using the Right Word, Comma Between the Day and the Year**

__________ of my friends were born on July 16 2000.
(To, Two, Too)

- **Using the Right Word, Comma Between the Day and the Year**

Vacation __________ our school begins June 8 2007.
(for, four)

- **Using the Right Word, Comma Between the Day and the Year**

On May 25 2007, the circus will be __________.
(hear, here)

- **Using the Right Word, Comma Between the Day and the Year**

Did you __________ the class trip is on March 1 2007?
(hear, here)

- **Using the Right Word, Comma Between the Day and the Year**

Grannie was sixty-__________ on August 22 2006!
(for, four)

Week 36: Corrected Sentences

- **Using the Right Word, Comma Between the Day and the Year**

Two
_________ of my friends were born on July 16, 2000.
(To, Two, Too)

- **Using the Right Word, Comma Between the Day and the Year**

Vacation ___for___ our school begins June 8, 2007.
(for, four)

- **Using the Right Word, Comma Between the Day and the Year**

On May 25, 2007, the circus will be ___here___ .
(hear, here)

- **Using the Right Word, Comma Between the Day and the Year**

Did you ___hear___ the class trip is on March 1, 2007?
(hear, here)

- **Using the Right Word, Comma Between the Day and the Year**

Grannie was sixty-___four___ on August 22, 2006!
(for, four)

MUG Shot Paragraphs

The MUG Shot paragraphs are a quick and efficient way to review mechanics, usage, and grammar errors each week. These paragraphs also serve as proofreading exercises. Each paragraph can be corrected and discussed in 8 to 10 minutes.

Implementation and Evaluation

The sets of MUG Shot sentences for the second semester have corresponding MUG Shot paragraphs. Each of the first 9 MUG Shot paragraphs (weeks 19–27) focuses on the same skill addressed in the sentences for the corresponding week. Each of the remaining 9 paragraphs (weeks 28–36) features the two skills covered in the corresponding week's mixed-review sentences.

Implementation

During the second half of the year, MUG Shot paragraphs can be implemented at the end of the week, as a review or as an evaluation. This can be done orally as a whole class activity, or you may choose to distribute copies of the week's paragraph, read it aloud, and then have students make their own corrections. Afterward, go over the paragraph as a class to make sure that everyone knows what the changes are and why they are necessary. (You may want to refer to the corresponding MUG Shot sentences during your discussion.)

Evaluation

If you use the paragraphs as an evaluation activity, we recommend that you give students a score reflecting the number of changes the student has marked correctly (before or after any discussion). Use this information to guide individual instruction.

Week 19: A Tortoise

- **Comma Between the Day and the Year**

Harriet the tortoise lives in the Australian Zoo. She turned 175 years old on November 15 2005. She will be 200 years old on November 15 2030. She is one of the oldest living animals on earth!

Week 19: Corrected Paragraph

Harriet the tortoise lives in the Australian Zoo. She turned 175 years old on November 15, 2005. She will be 200 years old on November 15, 2030. She is one of the oldest living animals on earth!

Week 20: Buzz, Pound, Bang!

- **Comma Between Words in a Series**

Dad was building a doghouse. I was helping him. I carried his hammer nails and saw. We worked very hard. Then we had soup crackers and cheese.

Week 20: Corrected Paragraph

Dad was building a doghouse. I was helping him. I carried his hammer, nails, and saw. We worked very hard. Then we had soup, crackers, and cheese.

Week 21: A Hot, Hot Day

- **Apostrophe to Make a Contraction**

The sun is shining. Im going to put on my hat and sunglasses. I cant forget my sunscreen. Im ready to go!

Week 21: Corrected Paragraph

The sun is shining. I'm going to put on my hat and sunglasses. I can't forget my sunscreen. I'm ready to go!

Week 22: To Market, to Market

- **Using the Right Word (buy, by)**

Dad takes me to __________ milk, cheese,
(buy, by)

and bread. We pass __________ my friend's house.
(buy, by)

She lives __________ the store.
(buy, by)

Week 22: Corrected Paragraph

Dad takes me to buy milk, cheese,
(buy, by)

and bread. We pass by my friend's house.
(buy, by)

She lives by the store.
(buy, by)

Week 23: Road Closed!

- **Using the Right Word (road, rode)**

Yesterday, I ____________ my bike. The
(road, rode)

____________ was bumpy. I hope workers will fix
(road, rode)

that ____________ soon.
(road, rode)

Week 23: Corrected Paragraph

Yesterday, I rode my bike. The
(road, rode)

road was bumpy. I hope workers will fix
(road, rode)

that road soon.
(road, rode)

Week 24: A Special House

- **Using the Right Word (for, four)**

Dad built a little house ____________ butterflies.
(for, four)
He made it ____________ our backyard. Mom planted
(for, four)
special plants. The next day ____________ blue
(for, four)
butterflies came to the house.

Week 24: Corrected Paragraph

Dad built a little house for butterflies.
(for, four)
He made it for our backyard. Mom planted
(for, four)
special plants. The next day four blue
(for, four)
butterflies came to the house.

Week 25: April Showers Bring May Flowers

- **Using the Right Word (know, no)**

There are ________ *(know, no)* flowers in our yard. I think I ________ *(know, no)* why. ________ *(Know, No)* rain fell for a long time. We also have ________ *(know, no)* shade in the yard. Do you ________ *(know, no)* what we can do?

Week 25: Corrected Paragraph

There are no *(know, no)* flowers in our yard. I think I know *(know, no)* why. No *(Know, No)* rain fell for a long time. We also have no *(know, no)* shade in the yard. Do you know *(know, no)* what we can do?

Week 26: Listen, Listen

- **Using the Right Word (hear, here)**

__________ we are in the mountains.
(Hear, Here)

We can camp __________. Listen, you can
(hear, here)

__________ the rushing river. Do you __________
(hear, here) (hear, here)

the owls hooting?

Week 26: Corrected Paragraph

Here we are in the mountains.
(Hear, Here)

We can camp here. Listen, you can
(hear, here)

hear the rushing river. Do you hear
(hear, here) (hear, here)

the owls hooting?

Week 27: Breakfast Outing

- **Using the Right Word (to, two, too)**

Grandma took me ____________ a restaurant.
(to, two, too)

We ordered ____________ glasses of milk. I had
(to, two, too)

blueberry pancakes, ____________ . Everything was
(to, two, too)

yummy! I think I ate ____________ much.
(to, two, too)

Week 27: Corrected Paragraph

Grandma took me ___to___ a restaurant.
(to, two, too)

We ordered ___two___ glasses of milk. I had
(to, two, too)

blueberry pancakes, ___too___ . Everything was
(to, two, too)

yummy! I think I ate ___too___ much.
(to, two, too)

Week 28: Summer Storm

- **Capital Letter for the First Word in a Sentence, Using the Right Word**

I see big, black clouds. ____________ *(Hear, Here)* comes the rain. it is raining ____________ *(to, two, too)* hard. run ____________ *(for, four)* cover! look at the lightning. can you ____________ *(hear, here)* thunder? This is a big storm.

Week 28: Corrected Paragraph

I see big, black clouds. Here *(Hear, Here)* comes the rain. I it is raining too *(to, two, too)* hard. R run for *(for, four)* cover! L look at the lightning. C can you hear *(hear, here)* thunder? This is a big storm.

Week 29: Show-and-Tell

- **Period, Question Mark, or Exclamation Point; Capital Letters for Special Names**

Today is show-and-tell day Do you want to see my special rock My friend maria has a new book What does carlos have in his brown bag Wow, it is space food We like to share our special things

Week 29: Corrected Paragraph

Today is show-and-tell day. Do you want to see my special rock? My friend Maria has a new book. What does Carlos have in his brown bag? Wow, it is space food! We like to share our special things.

Week 30: Treasure

- **Capital Letter for the Word *I*, Question Mark**

i am going on a treasure hunt! Will i get my own map Do i need to take a flashlight Will I get to keep the treasure May i ask Libby to come along i hope we can find the treasure.

Week 30: Corrected Paragraph

i am going on a treasure hunt! Will i get my own map Do i need to take a flashlight Will I get to keep the treasure May i ask Libby to come along i hope we can find the treasure.

Week 31: Our Lost Dog

- **Apostrophe to Make a Contraction, Exclamation Point**

Our dog Dutch was missing I said, "Im going to look for him." My friend said hed come, too. Then we saw Dutch coming up the sidewalk. We were very happy. Lets go home, Dutch

Week 31: Corrected Paragraph

Our dog Dutch was missing! I said, "I'm going to look for him." My friend said he'd come, too. Then we saw Dutch coming up the sidewalk. We were very happy. Let's go home, Dutch!

Week 32: A Fun Day

- **Apostrophe to Make a Contraction, Plurals That Add *-s***

I cant wait to play with my two friend. Well ride bike, fly kite, and eat grape. Maybe youd like to play with us.

Week 32: Corrected Paragraph

I can't wait to play with my two friends. We'll ride bikes, fly kites, and eat grapes. Maybe you'd like to play with us.

Week 33: Go Fetch!

- **Period After an Abbreviation**

"Where is the baseball?" asked Kyle. "Did it fly into Mrs Gray's yard?" "No, but look, here comes Mr Brown's dog," said Jeb. "He has the baseball in his mouth." "Good catch!" shouted Mr Brown.

Week 33: Corrected Paragraph

"Where is the baseball?" asked Kyle. "Did it fly into Mrs⊙Gray's yard?" "No, but look, here comes Mr⊙Brown's dog," said Jeb. "He has the baseball in his mouth." "Good catch!" shouted Mr⊙Brown.

Week 34: Class Trip

- **Plurals That Add *-s*, Comma After the Greeting and the Closing in a Letter**

Dear Aunt Eve

My class went to a museum. We walked through a rain forest with big tree. One case showed a hundred different bug. There were many kinds of bird shown, too. We learned a lot!

Love

Benny

Week 34: Corrected Paragraph

Dear Aunt Eve,

My class went to a museum. We walked through a rain forest with big trees. One case showed a hundred different bugs. There were many kinds of birds shown, too. We learned a lot!

Love,

Benny

Week 35: Grocery Shopping

- **Comma Between Words in a Series**

Mr. March goes to the grocery store. He buys bananas eggs lettuce and butter. He pays the clerk. She gives him quarters dimes and pennies in change. He says, "Thank you very much."

Week 35: Corrected Paragraph

Mr. March goes to the grocery store. He buys bananas, eggs, lettuce, and butter. He pays the clerk. She gives him quarters, dimes, and pennies in change. He says, "Thank you very much."

Week 36: Spring Wedding

- **Using the Right Word, Comma Between the Day and the Year**

On May 8 2005, ____________ (to, two, too) people got married. I was in the wedding. I had ____________ (to, two, too) get all dressed up. ____________ (For, Four) other people were in the wedding, ____________ (to, two, too). It was fun!

Week 36: Corrected Paragraph

On May 8, 2005, two (to, two, too) people got married. I was in the wedding. I had to (to, two, too) get all dressed up. Four (For, Four) other people were in the wedding, too (to, two, too). It was fun!

Writing Practice

This section offers two types of writing practice. The freewriting done in response to the writing prompts can be shared in follow-up sessions and later shaped into finished writing. The list of writing topics will tap the memories of your students and support personal journal writing.

Writing Prompts

Introducing Writing Prompts

Remind students that they can become better writers by practicing every day. Writing in journals and diaries is one way to do this. Sometimes it helps to have a starting point for daily writing. These writing starters are often called writing prompts.

Forms of Writing Prompts

Writing prompts use a variety of starting points.

Pictures • Pictures can remind students of something they have seen or done or a place they have been. Talking about a picture or allowing students to talk briefly with a partner will help them get started.

Possible Titles • Discuss some of the different ideas evoked by the same title. This demonstrates the students' freedom to take off in their own directions.

Sentence Starters • Introduce sentence starters by doing some orally in class. Stress that there are no right answers. If students have several good ideas, tell them that they may want to keep track of these for later writing practice.

Questions • Questions naturally prompt written responses. They may also serve as possible titles.

Note: Remember that the purpose of a prompt is to get the flow of words started. The finished writing may be quite removed from the original prompt. (If you wish to have students respond specifically to a prompt, make that clear to them.)

Think and Write

First, have students look at the writing prompt and think about it. As soon as they get an idea, they should start writing. Have them keep writing until they run out of ideas or come to the end of their stories.

Time to Stop!

Ask students to write for a certain amount of time. It may be helpful to tell them when the time is nearly over.

Share

Students often enjoy sharing their writing with one another. Set aside time for students to read their writing to a partner or the class. Sharing writing soon after it is finished, while it is still fresh in their minds, may be the best plan for young writers. Have students color the pictures on the writing-prompt pages for a bulletin-board display.

Save Your Writing

Writing prompts may give students good story ideas or start them thinking about other writing topics. Set up a place for students to save their writing so that they can come back to it later.

One Special Day

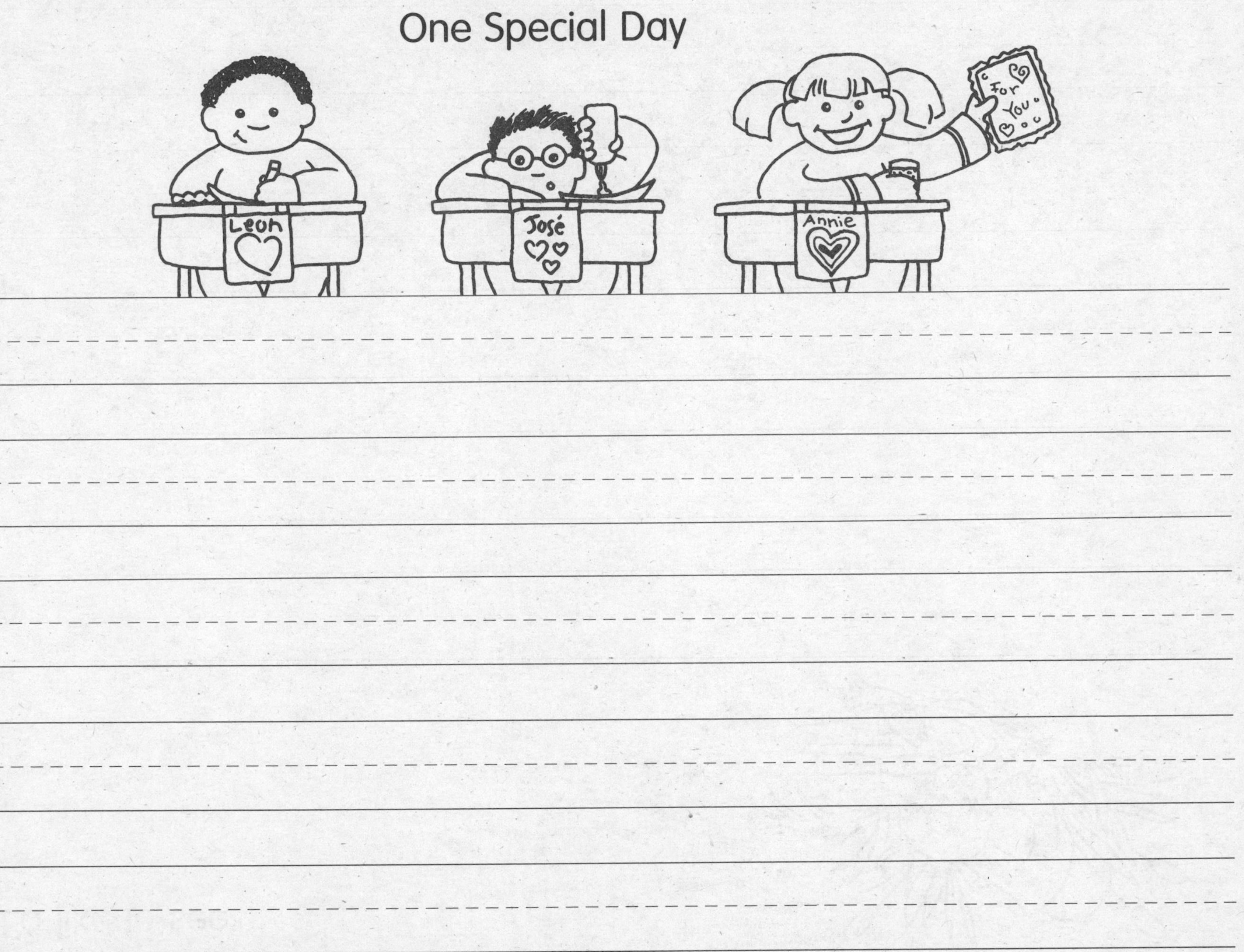

I'd like to see . . .

Noisy Times and Quiet Times

I like to make . . .

What if toys could talk?

My Shopping List
yo-yo
jump rope
paint set

Don't litter!

Big Pets and Small Pets

Insects, Insects Everywhere

I'm happy when . . .

How Plants Grow

My Adventure

My Favorite Foods

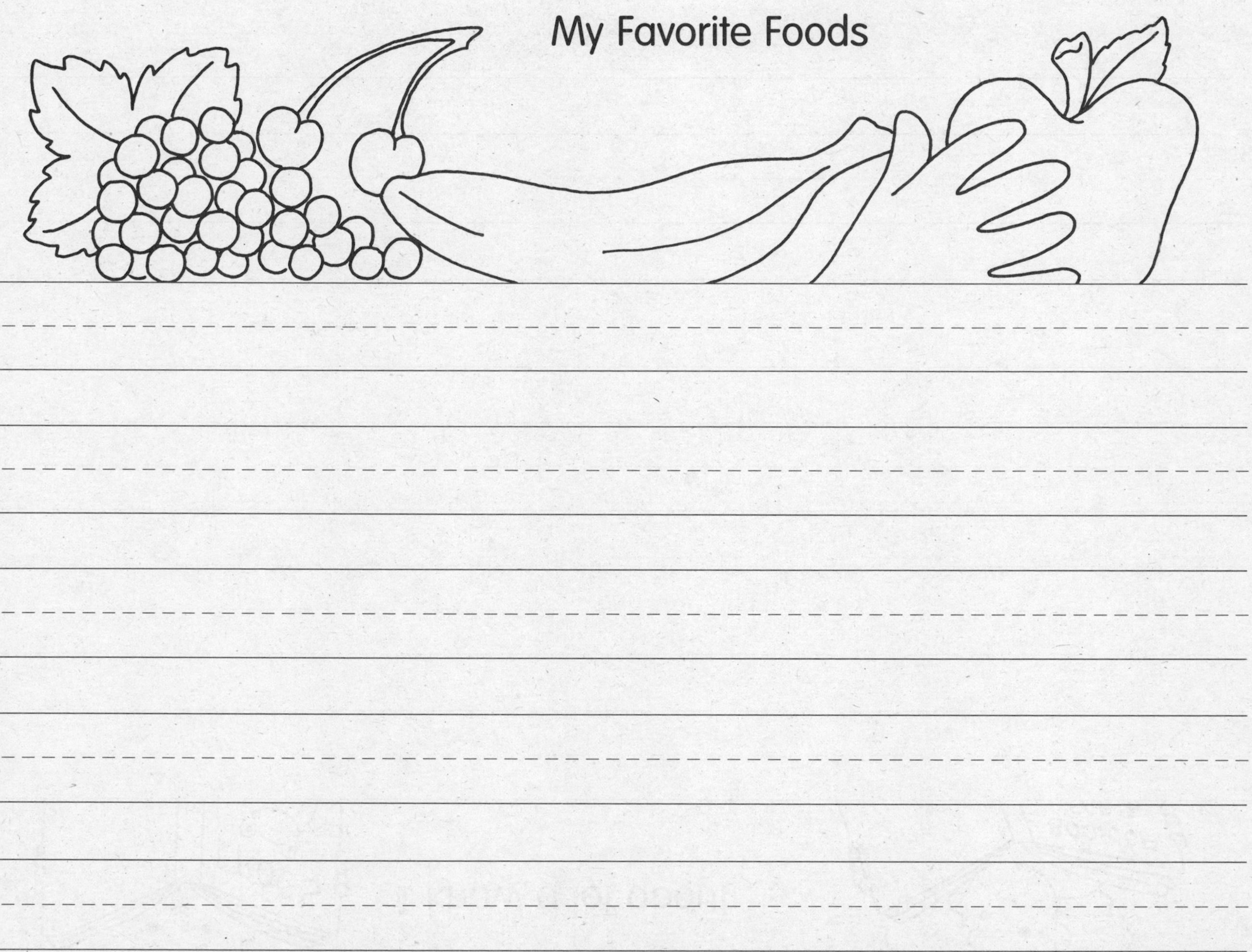

I know a lot about . . .

Picnic Fun

Who's at the zoo?

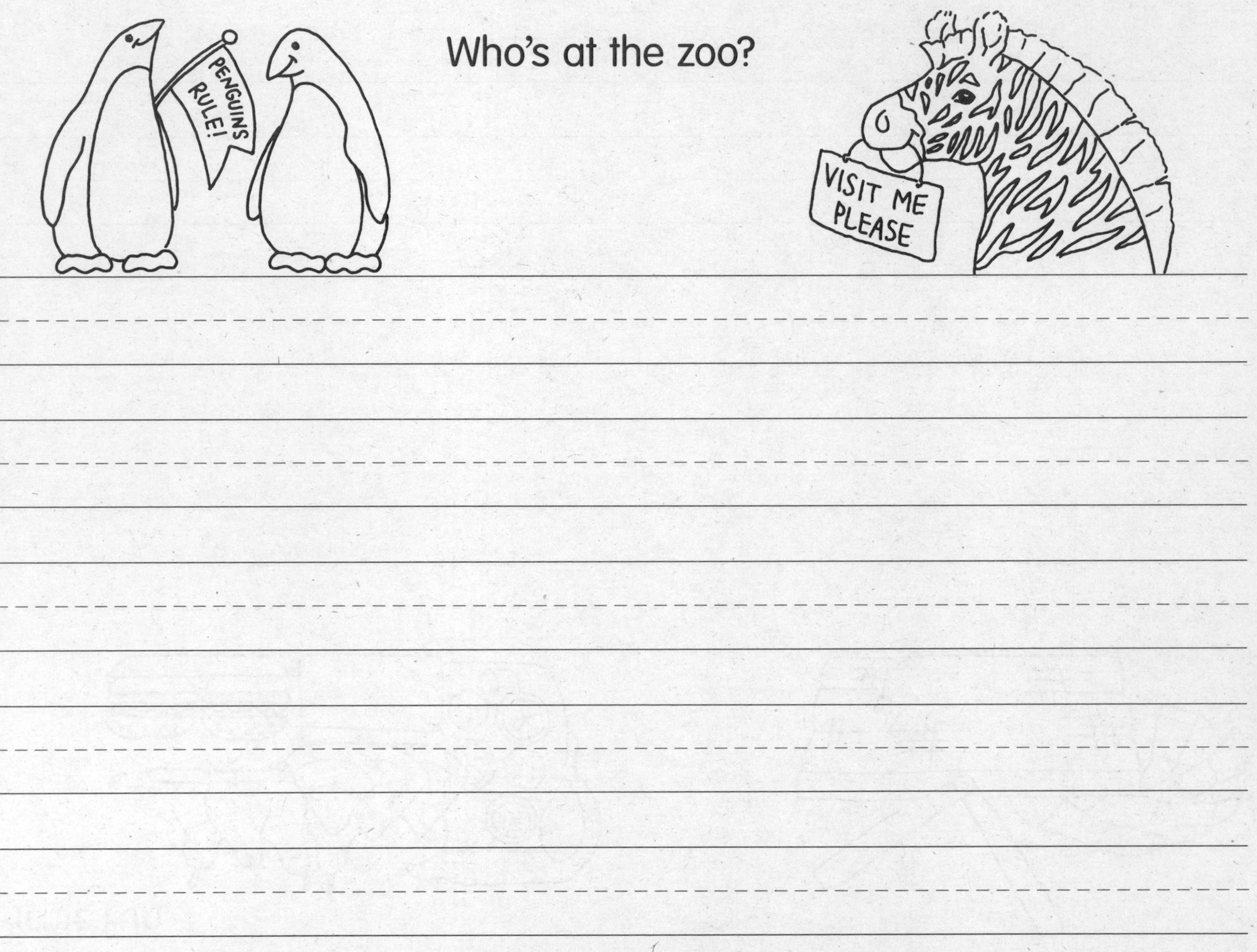

What will I share?

I rode on a . . .

The Parade

Why is the sky blue?

Why is the sun so bright?

I wonder why . . .

What's under my bed?

What if I were 10 years old?

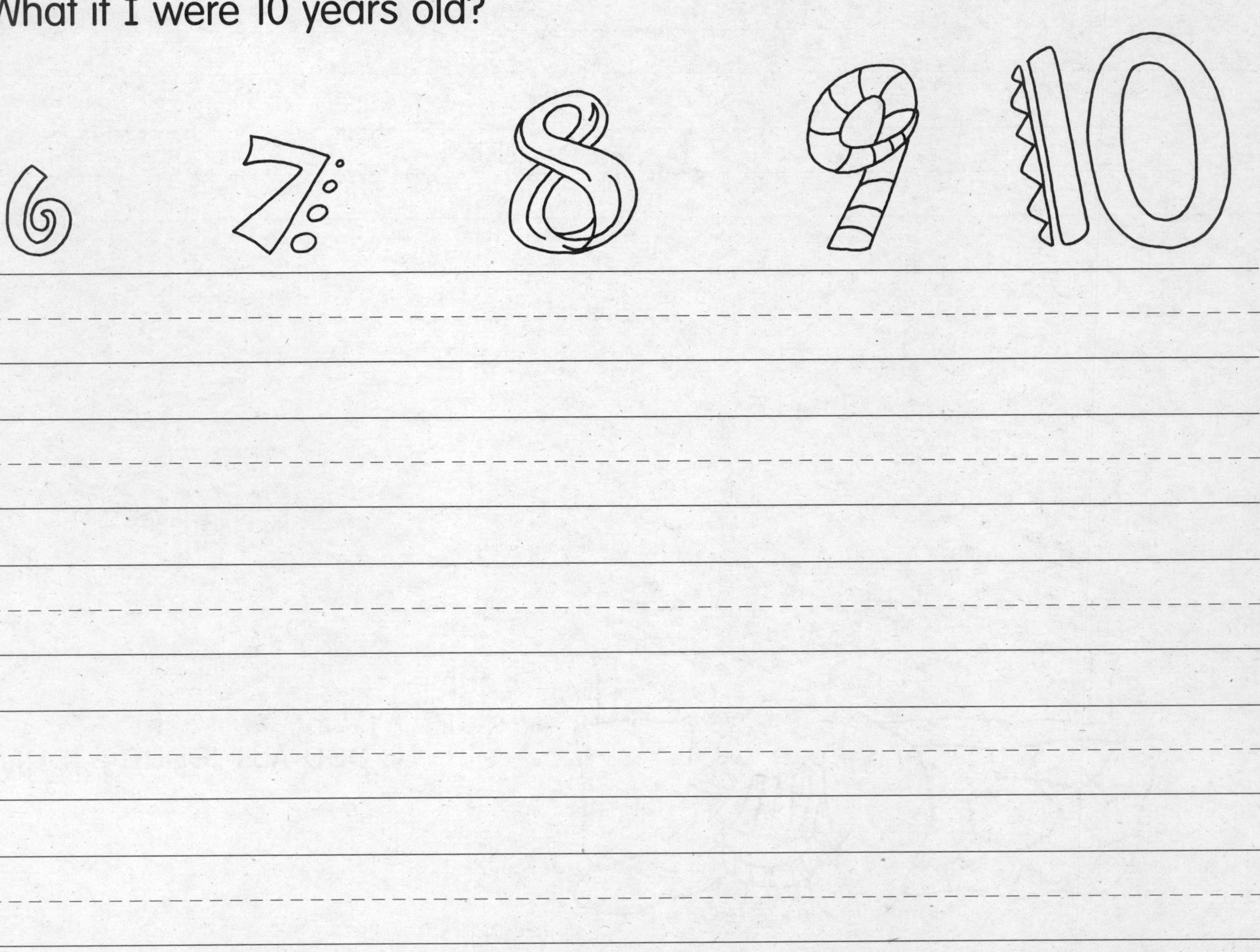

What makes me laugh?

My Chores

Working Together

Colors

I wish . . .

Story Time
FAIRY TALES

If I had a garden . . .

When I dream . . .

One day, it was so hot . . .

If I were the president . . .

What if . . . ?

If I could play on the moon . . .

What if you could fly?

If I could be an animal . . .

The Best Recess Ever

Once, it was so cold . . .

If I could go anywhere . . .

The best hiding spot . . .

How to . . .

This is a digital slideshow about my dog.

Writing Topics

"I can tap into [my students'] human instinct to write if I help them realize that their lives and memories are worth telling stories about, and if I help them zoom in on topics of fundamental importance to them."

—writing teacher JUNE GOULD

As a classroom teacher, you have the ability to instill young learners with a love of writing. Incorporate writing into your daily classroom routine. Here's one way to develop an effective program.

Getting Started

At the beginning of the school year, introduce in-class journal writing. The most effective way to get students into writing is simply to let them write often and freely about their own lives, without having to worry about grades or turning their writing in. This helps them develop a feel for "real" writing—writing that comes from their own thoughts and feelings.

Personal Journals

Personal journals provide a great opportunity for students to write candidly. (And no other type of writing is so easy to implement.) All your students need are notebooks and pencils. You provide the time to write and the encouragement to explore whatever is on their minds.

Writing Topics

To begin, provide your students with several personal writing topics. The students may use these as a starting point or write about something else entirely. The choice is theirs. (Pages of suggested topic ideas are found in this book on pages 146–155.) You may wish to reproduce these topic sheets for students to keep in their portfolios.

Writing Schedule

Writing schedules can be flexible. In some classrooms, students write every day for 5 to 10 minutes when they get to school. Sometimes, students journal when they come back to the classroom after lunch. The time of day is not important, but getting into a writing routine is invaluable. Of course, the schedule may vary at times; and as a teacher you need to cash in on "teachable moments." Think of the ways you can connect writing and journaling throughout the curriculum.

Keep It Going

It is so important that students develop a comfort for the writing process. They should not be judged, therefore, on the journal as a product. Journal time should be based on participation. If students write and try, it should be considered a success.

Writing Topics

- **Five Senses**
  A breezy day
  Creepy noises
  Slurping spaghetti
  Hammers and nails
  The hottest day
  A beautiful sight
  The yummiest lunch
  The smell I like best
  It looks like . . .
  It feels like . . .
  Quiet sounds
  As cold as . . .

Writing Topics

- **Food**

Breakfast
Picnics
The perfect meal
Cooking at home
My favorite aisle in the grocery store
If I could order anything . . .
One food I can't eat
If I owned a restaurant, my menu would be . . .
Favorite fruits

Writing Topics

- **Special Days**

  Thanksgiving dinner
  Winter holidays
  The Fourth of July parade
  Holiday decorations
  New Year's traditions
  Holiday foods
  Homemade presents
  Holiday greeting cards
  Family picnics
  Traditional celebrations I enjoy

Writing Topics

- **Other Ideas**

The sandbox
My favorite hiding place
Craft day
A silly day
A funny day
Winter adventures
My travels
My pet
Dreams
Skateboarding
Sand castles
When I grow up . . .

Writing Topics

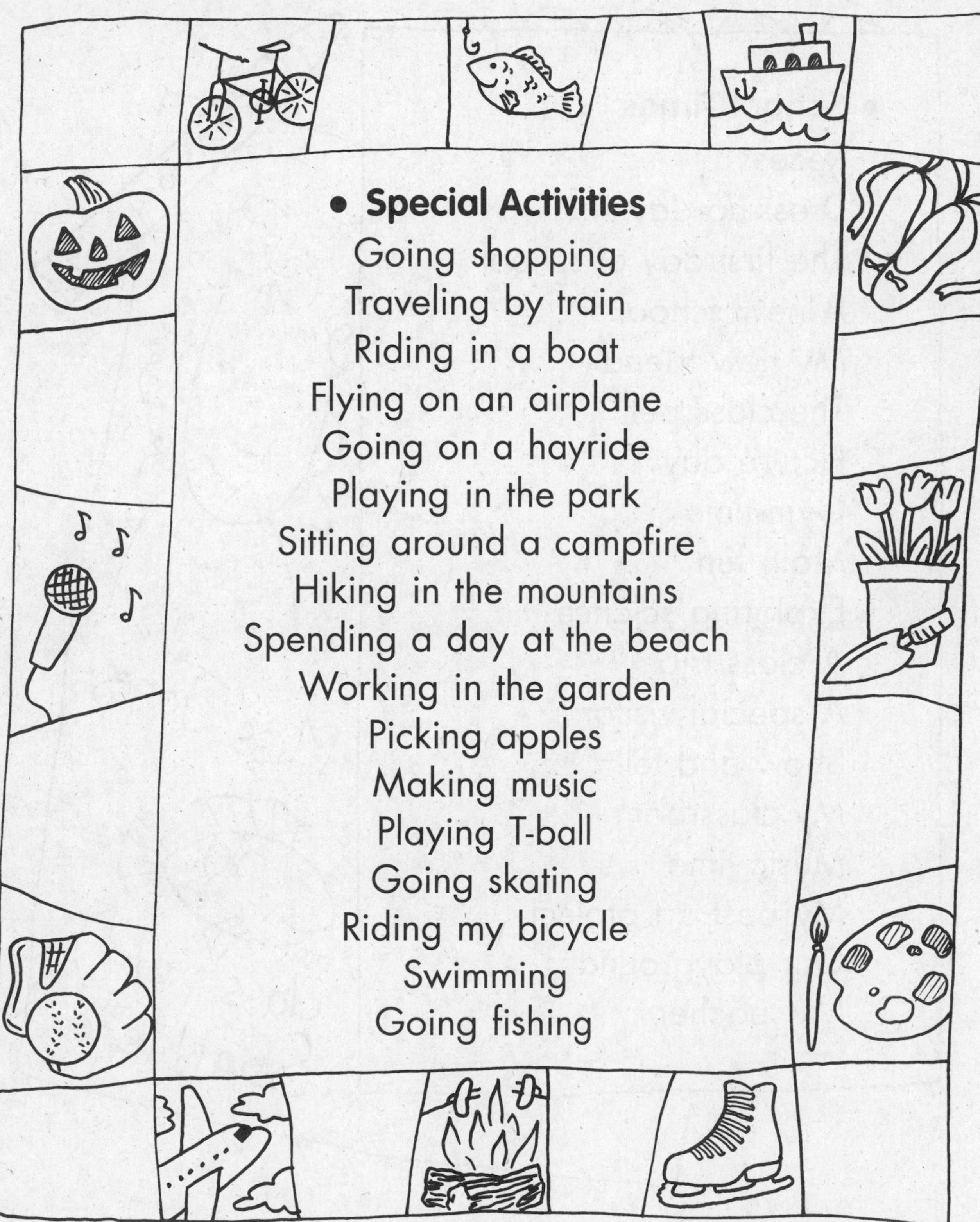

- **Special Activities**

Going shopping
Traveling by train
Riding in a boat
Flying on an airplane
Going on a hayride
Playing in the park
Sitting around a campfire
Hiking in the mountains
Spending a day at the beach
Working in the garden
Picking apples
Making music
Playing T-ball
Going skating
Riding my bicycle
Swimming
Going fishing

Writing Topics

- **School Times**

  Recess
  Dress-up day
  The first day of school
  A new school
  My new friend
  The class pet
  Picture day
  Gym time
  Math fun
  Exploring science
  A class trip
  A special visitor
  Show and tell
  My classroom
  Music time
  My best art project
  Our playground
  My teacher

Writing Topics

- **Things I Like**

Seeing bright colors
Visiting big cities
Swimming in lakes
Singing
Laughing
Helping
Learning
Fishing
Camping
Running and jumping
Climbing
Hiking
Dancing
Being with grown-ups
Using computers
Planting trees
Fixing things
Playing games
Reading
Drawing

Writing Topics

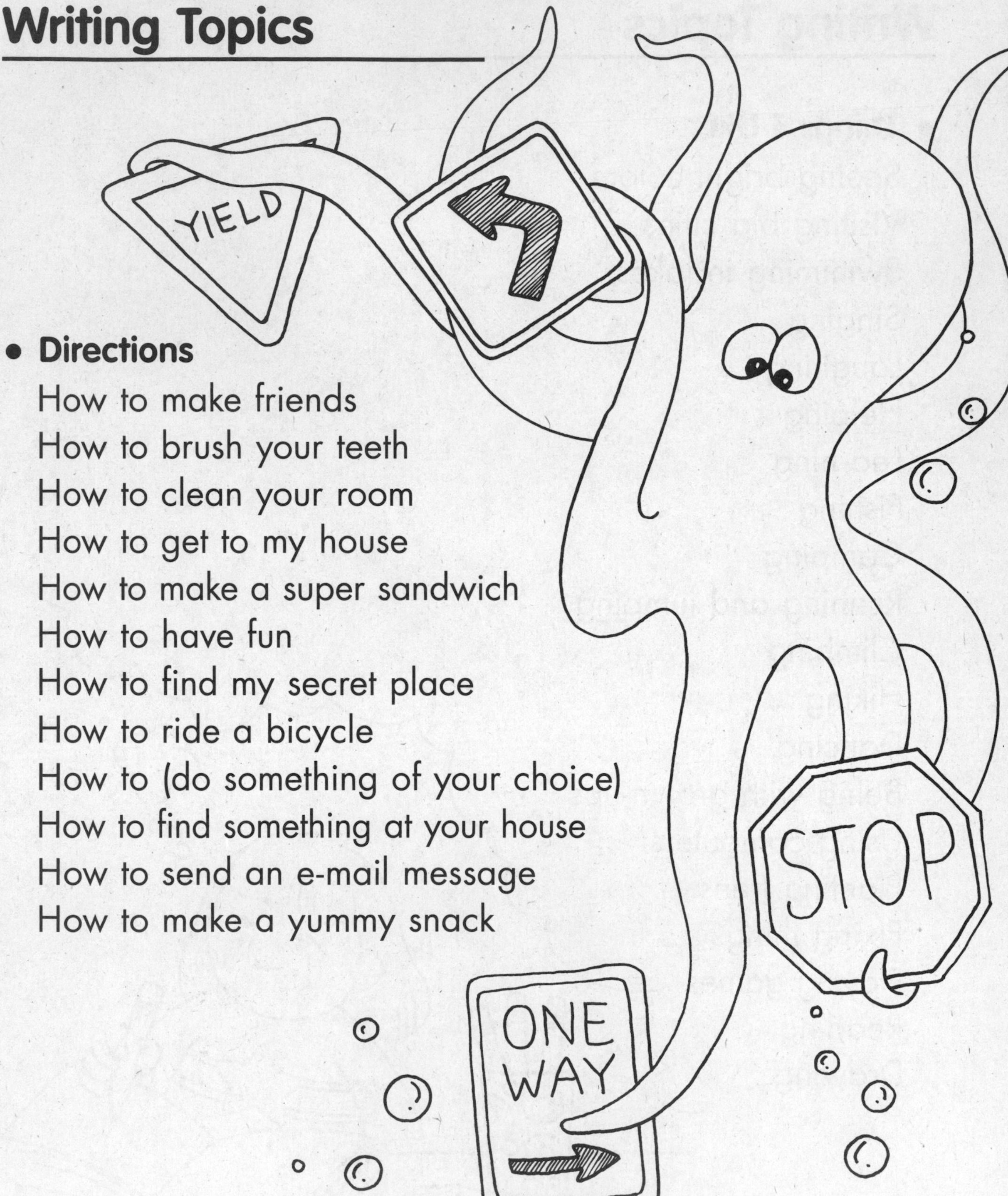

- **Directions**

How to make friends
How to brush your teeth
How to clean your room
How to get to my house
How to make a super sandwich
How to have fun
How to find my secret place
How to ride a bicycle
How to (do something of your choice)
How to find something at your house
How to send an e-mail message
How to make a yummy snack

Writing Topics

- **Interesting People**

  My mom or dad
  A brother or sister
  My teacher
  Our principal
  My friend
  My pet
  The president
  A neighbor
  The bus driver
  A television news reporter
  A professional athlete
  or performer
  (Someone of your choice)

Writing Topics

- **Things I'd Like to Be**

  Bird
  Dog
  Baby animal
  Ocean animal
  Desert animal
  Water animal
  Cat
  Bear
  (Animal of your choice)
  Car
  Sound
  Color
  Feather
  Toy
  Instrument
  (Object of your choice)

Writing Topics

- **Interesting Places to Go**

Grandma's house
The moon
A space station
Another country
The Statue of Liberty
The seashore
A mountaintop
The White House
The Grand Canyon
A park
A movie
My friend's house
A big city
The circus
A museum
The zoo
The state capital
The library

Writing Topics

- **Things I Like to Make**

pinatas
balloon animals
clay sculptures
play dough
origami
finger puppets
rock animals
scrap books
bead jewelry
paintings
bird houses
model cars
paper airplanes
suncatchers
holiday decorations
treehouses
snow forts
dioramas
masks
mobiles
kites